THE WAY SUMMER ENDS

poems

Thomas Mitchell

LOST HORSE PRESS
Sandpoint, Idaho

ACKNOWLEDGMENTS

Some of these poems have appeared in the following publications, and grateful acknowledgment is made to their editors:

Barataria
Borrowed Times
California Quarterly
Cloudbank
Cutbank
Inlet
Kentucky Review
New England Review
New Letters
Quarterly West
The Chariton Review
The New Orleans Review
Uzzano

"Directions to a Local Bar," "Seven Years of Snow," "We Who Need Sorrow," and "A Map Of Montana in Miami" also appeared in *Where We Are: The Montana Poets Anthology*.

Cover Art: Heidi Malott, *Crows' Autumn Feast,* 8" x 8" oil on masonite. Other paintings by
    Ms. Malott may be found online at www.heidimalott.com.
Author Photo: Don Bunyard.
Book & Cover Design: Christine Holbert.

FIRST EDITION

This and other LOST HORSE PRESS titles may be viewed online at www.losthorsepress.org.

LIBRARY OF CONGRESS CATALOGING-IN-PUBLICATION DATA
Names: Mitchell, Thomas, 1963- author.
Title: The way summer ends : poems / Thomas Mitchell.
Description: First edition. | Sandpoint, Idaho : Lost Horse Press, 2016.
Identifiers: LCCN 2016028098 | ISBN 9780996858434 (trade paper : alk. paper)
Subjects: LCSH: Summer—Poetry.
Classification: LCC PS3613.I8665 .A6 2016 | DDC 811/.6—dc23
LC record available at https://lccn.loc.gov/2016028098

THE WAY SUMMER ENDS

for Linda

We turn out the lamps between earth
and the stars. Our eyes fold up like acrobats,
muscular and tense. I dream you, you dream me.
The windows so bright, and the nails in the roof.
The moon, white on the backyard fence.
In the dark we see only with our fingers. Do you want
to know how our voices sing in the night?
Put back the dust. Announce the stars,
the death of stars, the history
of all the stars.

CONTENTS

I

II

III

I

NO MATTER HOW MUCH I TRY

Beyond the trees, frogs sing in syncopation
to the stars, porch lights come on one by one.
The crows rocking on the powerline have nothing to do
as the flicker of passing headlights fades away.

Alone, by the window, things almost seem right
and darkness is enough to keep me awake. I've done this
more than once, and I know if I look away,
everything will disappear.

It's getting late and the riffs of jazz passing through my head don't help.
The moon doesn't help, half-hidden back behind the clouds.
And if I walked where would I walk? No matter how much
I want to move on, the rhythm of the river comes back pulsing
in the light of the stars.

Somewhere, less than a mile away, Isabella Juarez is turning
in her sleep, a woman turning in her own passion, a woman who talks
to herself and believes in tomorrow, believes in the lies.

By dawn
The arm of the mimosa tree juts perpendicular
across the lawn and rests in a shadow on the window.

THE ARGUMENT

All I wanted was to think about the girl I saw yesterday,
dragging a kite against the sky, but somehow the rain,
gentle at first, then persistent, already pooling in the driveway
by the fence, changed all that, and she started to speak
about what we had known for days

without saying, and her words steady, turning soft
as the weather. It wasn't just about us anymore.
The rusty bicycle against the garage was all I could see
for now, the chain dangling, dropping off to one side,
like a broken conversation.

Before long the rain let up, after falling for hours.
All I wanted was to lean into the window
quietly following the scrub jays making short order
of the thimbleberries at the edge of the fence,
then breaking toward the sky.

DECEMBER 27TH

This is a night that arrives like a strong wind from the South, rattles the gutters, swirling willow branches scratching the upstairs windows. There, in the corner of the livingroom, an ungainly spruce, the needles falling, a box of ornaments, most broken, by the glow of the heater. I don't want this to happen again: yesterday's breakfast dishes on the diningroom table. The empty coffee mugs. And now that you are gone, even the riffs of Dave Brubeck, spinning from the phonograph don't help, the pale winter moonlight shining through a gap in the garden fence doesn't help. As the high weeds throw their shadows across the yard, a white moth floats away from the window, and the bright lights drizzle off the front porch roof.

THE COVERLET

Only the flickerering lampshade
in the livingroom, a moth spiraling
around the incandescent light.
You, asleep on the sofa with the book
you were reading last night face down on the cushion.
We were listening to Quincy and Miles,
the last record still spins on the spindle.
Sometimes I say things that confuse even me.
I know you don't understand why.
If I waken you, what voice could I use
to explain, to let you know how little I understand
about the words that come between us.
It's cold; all I have is the coverlet you embroidered
with deep green evergreens.
I wrap it around you.

THE ESCHER HANDS

At night I awaken to inanimate hands, Escher hands, recreating themselves on the crazy quilt. Hands that cross each other, the hands of the departed. My Uncle Gene talked for hours to nasturtiums, pinching each nub between forefinger and thumb. Aunt Cela, her hands like clay on a potter's wheel, sculpted and formed with each turn, turning in grace. My mother's hands steady as her needlework, ocher threads trailing from her fingers, over her wrists. My father's hands, never clean, dark blemishes of diesel oil, indelible lines, scars from a broken valve line repair, marks infused by an overheated radiator, the tip of the left forefinger severed once from a spinning Studebaker fan blade, then again in our basement on his tablesaw. My bedroom door is ever so slightly ajar, constantly creaking, but when I look it's neither open wider, nor more closed. I guess it's just breathing air from the air conditioner. The window, partially open, inhales and exhales the plain white curtains. Alone in the dark, I know there are people no longer here; it doesn't make any difference what they are saying, or what the clock says, or that the solar system, the planets, might be as random as a circle of marbles, a circle of boys, or a handful of jacks scattered like stars on the pavement.

THUNDER

for Don Schofield

On the blue formica table, the *Beginner's Birdhouse* book,
upside down, leaning to one side, and nails, Phillips screws,
a yellow-handled screwdriver, a small claw hammer.
You've left me coffee, two biscuits on the granite countertop.
What is it that holds us together? Last night you reached over,
touched my hand, and before I opened my eyes,
I could hear the rain, soft thunder against the curtains.

NECKLACES

for Laura Landberg

Alone by the window, she waits for something,
anything to happen, then puts down her needle and thread,
the half finished embroidery of Androcles and the Lion.
Trailing scarlet and ocher threads, she leads me by the hand
through the moonlight where we follow the stars
to the edge of the garden, where with little effort
a snail becomes a cartouche, a perilous white moth
beats its wings softly on the window. These are the
nights that come on their own, when the shoulder
of the Mimosa gently rubs against the kitchen eave and
with her left hand, she lifts the hostia, turning a leaf's edge,
as seven tiny aphids cascade
like a necklace of shiny green beads.

RAIN FALLING ON RAIN

for Kaaren Reiche

Sparrows are dipping in the empty sky,
a steady wind shakes the acacia tree.

How quiet the world can be, between the rain
and the easterly moving clouds.

If you watch the window long enough, the usual squirrel
winds around the feeder.

The sound of steam slowly rises from the radiator,
and you begin to understand

the scattering of wrens crossing the lawn,
negotiating the madrone, one branch, then another.

HALLOWEEN, 2014

We've rescued the pumpkin from the front porch.
The cat is hiding somewhere in the garage. What is it
that makes children fascinated with the bones of the dead?
One flashlight after another brings them to our door;
the maniacal Chucky leers to one side, a smaller version
of the Cat in the Hat trips over the second step,
a princess bows and pirouettes, then leaves in a fit of giggles.

Maybe all dreams are anecdotal. I remember Madeline
who couldn't sleep without medication, a pistol by her side,
she saw the image of Christ in a window and shot away.
And I remember at fourteen longing for a girl named Evelyn.
She skated like an angel on the ice. In my mind our bodies
still turn in the darkness like a pale waltz.
The skeleton at the door demands chocolate or a caramel apple.

In this weather the arcing moon seems misaligned, the crows
return once again to their black mischief. I look beyond the sky
filled with miles of dark clouds, and the light of a broken
moon traces Evelyn's name on the lake's hard surface.

RETURN TO THE DANCE

Now that the sun
has gone around the house,
    the garden spiders spin their webs,
        shadows start to lengthen.

    A pair of cedar waxwings
glides across the river,
    then returns to the same branch.

    The dusting of snow
blankets the wild grapevines,

        powders the tangle of papery shells,
burst pods, and interlocking stalks.

    As lights come on one by one,
I watch you dance across the portico
        in the spectral moonlight,

and soon the pirouettes, the arabesque,
        are part of you again.

WHEN THE WIND IS RIGHT

for Martha Evans

We follow the moonlight through fields of bent alfalfa,
find the hayrick abandoned, lost in a tangle of blackberries,
    the cicadas already complaining,
and when the wind is right, we are two barn owls
    circling a stand of twisted oaks,
settling on a broken nob,
    our outstretched wings folding inward,
heads bobbing.

RECONCILIATION

What keeps me up this tender night:
the rattle and pull of the wind,
the tattered shards of a Japanese lantern,
the crow's slow departure from the crooked
branch. I can still see you, my father, drinking
on the patio where the moon grows dark
shimmering in a whiskey glass, the sweet
embrace of the evening hushes away loneliness.
If only I knew how to tell you swallows still fly
under the Folsom bridge, the rustling cottonwoods
turn yellow each autumn, and your bicycle, where you left it,
leans against the garage door. If only I knew how to show you
the glimmering bay where the late tide breaks,
wandering gulls searching the coastline,
broken shells turning on the shore.
The clouds spin quietly away from the horizon
and your grandson, like you, glances homeward
every few steps.

IN RESPONSE TO A DREAM

As I break twigs in the woods
near my house they pass through my hands,
as tiny sculptures intimate as Rodin,
Michelangelo, Dali . . . an empty chair,
a dismantled clock, its wheels and teeth forever
disconnected. I am wearing my father's
oversized wool coat, my mother's gold
band so tight on my ring finger I can
only turn it counterclockwise and remember
you, my father, my small hand in yours.
Along the riverbank of the American,
we paused and watched the false snow
of the cottonwoods, then scaled the tailings
of so much fool's gold across the river's surface.
Was that the summer I could not understand
why you rushed to the garden swooping
me in one arm, and a rainbow of gladiolas
in the other? Those nights, with my brother Boone,
the three of us assembled an impossible puzzle of slats
from old orange crates into the form of a canoe,
stretched canvas and got high from the paint and epoxy.

TAPESTRY

for Thomas Aslin

In April I resurrect a distant memory:
the shifting wind's persistent song,
my mother's graceful movements
as she threads away the morning clouds,
weaves a tapestry in the light
that lifts the fog from the river.

Two mallards flash across the river's
surface, fade in the distance
across the shadow of passing clouds.
A meadowlark sings the forgotten melody,
a song that haunts me late into the night.
The hour demands some semblance of grace.

Behind the window a drifting curtain graces
the darkening room, deep as the river
it flows and ebbs to the rhythm of the night.
So many times I've recalled this memory,
the melody of a recurring song,
the image of my mother in the clouds.

Then the moon slips beneath the clouds
and, reluctantly, they fall from grace,
the anxious call of the mockingbird's song,
the anxiety of the drifting river,
the loneliness I will always remember, takes
the silence from the night.

In another town, another broken night,
Jacinta Caballero traces clouds

in her whiskey glass, and with a gentle grace
negotiates the room, dancing like the river,
a dream no one knows,
forgotten in the cadence of song.

I turn on the radio to a familiar song:
The Five Satins' "In the Still of the Night."
Outside the fish are following the river
to some unknown destination. The clouds
surrender to the moon's pale grace,
the mallards just a flickery memory.

In the light of so many stars, clouds reshape themselves,
night becomes a Silvertone transitor radio, headlights
flashing like memories along the levee road.

OPEN RANGE

Captivated by the strange, buzzing
movement of the fluorescent desk lamp,
the wallpaper gives back the familiar
blue-gray pattern, hounds-on-the-track-
of-a-hare, and I lose myself, momentarily,
gazing at the intricate maneuvers
of the horsemen, the horses, vaulting
various schoolboy fancies, fences,
rows of pale green shrubbery. There's
a breeze, perfectly flat like paper,
that doesn't rustle the motionless mane
of each horse, but sets the teaspoon
clicking on the surface of the desk,
draws my attention to the window,
the curtains shifting across the old moon
that climbs the clouds before I have time
to do something in life, to shove
my feet into a fire until the knee boots
are a brilliant red. The dogs, wagging
over a hill in the distance, are no more
than vague patches, their heads bobbing
in the moonlight. They know night
has blossomed into a living love,
and the walk home always seems longer.

HOME AGAIN

Alone, simply by wishing, I abandon myself
to the darkened evergreens, to the house
we moved from years ago. It rolls back
in the cold grass. All I want is to dream
my uncle asleep on the divan. I leave
the livingroom unfinished, the blades
on the electric fan move like thought.
Somewhere, far away in his room,
my brother wanders through
his stamp collection, one country
at a time. When he brings his eyes back
they're his own again. I'm ready to believe
the almanac. I'm ready to believe young girls,
the way the moon gravitates in their thighs.
Sally Walker, you are right, no matter how wrong
you might have been. I can see where the yard ends
and those dark thickets of the hill begin.
We live out there, whoever we are.

SEVEN YEARS OF SNOW

We slept through winter while snow shook
the windows on Mercy Street. Even now as I remember
her classical body, as I grow older listening to the dark
gathering itself and the years, I am too lonely without
alcohol. As soon as I say 'now,' it becomes 'then.'
Most portraits are lies. They never show the sadness
at home, the same coat hanging in the closet. They never
show the places we evacuate, the places we are secretly
saving. Even now I see her with my mind. Those fingers,
tense, anxious as an arrow. I halfway believe
I dreamed her. The slow drifting, call it snow,
covers the trees in the distance. So many boys
pelting the old man. If the years could return
he'd laugh at the pain. The streets are like women
forever changing. And the woman in the window
is still the same. At this moment everyone should stop
and feel the cool air.

MEMORIAL DAY, WYOMING

These sandy hills all look the same.
Birds pass in flurries,
some heading west, and others
circling the roadside table,
beside the largest silver maple.
We sit in the sun, my wife
and I, drinking coffee,
receiving its warmth.
The clouds rear effortlessly.

Brie hops on one leg from one
white chalked square to the next,
her braids flapping, her bright dress
and bracelets, flying like a song.
She drifts to the table
where the shadow of a tree
forms a thin cage,
and for an instant, in the brief
intermittent light, we have lost
her.

In the hum-drum movement of the car,
I lean back and watch the hills
speeding away from us, and the memory
of Brie in the motionless desert,
standing behind the table,
leaning forward on her wrists.

WINTER GARDEN

for Linda

Sometimes, in the early hours, there is a great distance,
when the call of wandering geese retreats to the East,
and there is nothing in the drifting sky, revolving stars,
but Artemis and a huge bear. Smothered in hoar frost,
a fretwork of stalks, branches, and creepers shelters
the quail along the edge of our fence. A lone sunflower,
fragile as ice, waits to bloom. I watch the kitchen door
open, steam rising from the cup of hot tea warming
your hands as you walk down the wooden steps,
through the winter garden, past the whitish nubs,
at the end of panicles, some bent over and broken.

THE WAY SUMMER ENDS

By evening, the live oaks
in their twisted architecture,
straddle the hillsides, the wind
weaving their branches,
silent as the movement of an owl in flight,
dark against the eaves,
circling the moon instead of trees.

I strike a match
and a mantle of stars
churns inside the Coleman lantern,
then swings across the lawn
convulsively.

It's hard to be at home in this darkness.

In the sanctuary of my corner workshop,
I can almost hear the broken light,
the half-drawn blinds, the slow dust gathering
in the halo of the lamp.

TALKING IT OVER

   I remember how my father poured cement, shaped this pavement
from simple religion. He was finished when 'it felt right,'
when he traced his initials, hard and irrevocable.
That's all changed—the sidewalk and the weeds,
the elm twice its size.

   We make good memories for ourselves. From the bones
of old houses, I give you this one window, this glass
where faces and names converge to hold us blinded
in a world shaped by the world.

   I remember how he poured a drink, then coughed at the stars
on the screen door. Again and again I hear his laughter.
Like an old piano, he kept to himself the darkest notes.
When he left, he left three half-emptied bottles
and a week's news on the front porch

SMALL CRAFT ADVISORY

Father died before my memory. The house was swallowed
in a new light, a kind of glory that works on you
like a sharp knife, cuts into you and carves
all that you are, all that you will ever be.

Mornings, it was so much night.
The kitchen window darkening the eastern hills.
My brother diving into his dreams. My mother's light,
the lamp's deep shade. The white runs slowly
from her fingers. How the house lies.

The music is forever. Chopin, I think.
She smiles at her fingers, her flying hands
soft like aviation. Even at this distance,
she looks beautiful. Think of her like this
for the next twenty years. Now return
to the kitchen lamp, a colored picture postcard,
the TV on the blink. It only takes a little time.

Time is like a Buick in perfect tune.
Driving the dark, the starter whines,
the engine catches and roars, the light
makes the great trees stand out
beard to beard across the lawn.
A small metal virgin stands on the moon
of the dashboard.

At 55 I begin to age. Whole towns pass by.
Same memory, same picture. The seat worn through
to the springs, moths knocking at the windows.
Still, I move the throttle farther. I'm going
home.

THE AFFAIR

When the liquor fails at two A.M.,
he polishes his drink, draws
some smoke, and leaves the bar
feeling expensive. If the moon rakes
through leaves curling by the roadside,
if the small light dances on the ignition key,
he doesn't notice. Three minutes down
Lark Boulevard, his blue Desoto pulls
to the curb. An evergreen gives birth
to a dark tree. His mind drifts
to a small stone hut where birds fly
in and out the shuttered windows.

JOY RIDE

for Blue Ballou

I would have sworn it was undulating—
the river making its own noise retreating
into the bamboo, but no, it was only me
and this woman I met in the middle of town,
a real daredevil cornering at full speed,
skirting dozens of ticky-tacky fruit stands,
some of them true masterpieces, each one
unique with bright misspelt signs,
wobbly display stands loaded with ripe
fruit and flapping canvas awnings.

Nightfall found us following the convertible
over its route of leaps and straddlings,
skipping curbs, whipping down the empty
streets. The road curved with us like a fast
rumor through creeping commercialism—Joe's
Place, The Rumpus Room, twenty years
of eloquent graffiti. Police sirens
crisscrossed the sky.

Even now I see the diving gas gauge,
the engine whining like a ghost of itself.
We coast to the river's edge. It's alive
and green as a papaya. The bamboo lets
everything through—shouts, noises,
even whispers.

HEARTS

I can't remember why you left your diamond ring
swirling in the candlelight on the kitchen table.
And near the sink, a grocery list, alphabet magnets,
the Valentine you embroidered, now in my hands,
as I make it my own, turn the heart
so that it's right side out, imagine I close the gap
with a blind stitch.

DIRECTIONS TO A LOCAL BAR

Despite appearances, despite hard lines
and mad cartography, this is not a topographical
map. This is a barroom mirror with faces.
How easily the blonde from Cincinnati
ran out of luck. Tonight she remembers rain
and traveling. Weather's the same,
unpredictable. And who sees,
against the roses, a pale photograph of Roberto Clemente?
Not the drunk, two shot glasses away from the door,
not the divorcee staring at the bruise on the wall.
Maps have legends too, legends that measure continents,
seas. In the late tide, a fisherman draws the moon
floundering in his net. Here, the bartender
pours a good drink and the world forgets.
The dwarf leans his chair back on two legs
and state workers lie to their wives.
Eddie Moran puts on his cap
and the door closes quietly on air behind him.

PORTRAITS

for David Jared

I

Her hair was streaked with silver, and around her eyes
a series of lines. There were the white dishes gleaming
in the dishrack, the kitchen window shining
like a mirror in the moonlight, the philadendron silent
and stillborn on the sill, the faucet dripping,
the lace curtains dedicated solely to defining light.
She was washing dishes, one at a time in a tub
full of water, and as she paused for a minute,
she was holding a glass, she was holding a glass,
when the record skipped on the old phonograph,
and she felt it slip from her hands. Fragments
scattered like stars across the kitchen floor.

II

As he brushed his hair away from his forehead,
the room came in, a photograph of his father,
placed at an odd angle over the fireplace.
There was no fire, yet the room was very light,
and the whiteness, now altogether actual, seeming to drift in,
like some wave, to make the room a space, an intention.
He went over to the window and left his breath
on the glass. All he could see were the headlights of a car
disappear down Mulhallen street. Somehow,
he would need to begin the work of sorting through
everything. The empty cardboard boxes open on the floor.
Later he pulled out a record, very worn and scratched,
placed it on the spindle, and turned on the phonograph.
Then he let his arms swing out in great circles,
and hummed to himself the sounds of Chopin.

III

He opened a can of Pabst and felt the beer
crawl over his tongue, then went out to the barn
which his father had moved and built again,
by himself, to be doing something in the Autumn.
And there it was, then, and maybe now,
what tribute he could put into so much wood,
for his son, that he could move and put up again
with his own hands. He stared up into the loft
where the hay was shining beneath the moonlight
creeping though the cracks in the barn roof.
He felt old. His hands were in better shape
than his father's had been, but he felt old
and forgotten like the barn.

NANTUCKET REVISITED

I'm not talking about love,
to hell with love. I'm talking
about her wristwatch thrown down
anyhow on the table, talking
about water in the sink running
over potato peels, her voice
like a knife on glass. This is
forgivable. After all, she is 87,
it's eleven o'clock at night, and
she knows the work is stupid, she
knows there is solace in the white
half-light where anything can happen.
Why should she be ashamed of her
old bedfellow, wearing a Navy belt buckle,
staring into the remains of a fire,
immutable, head thrown back and mouth
open, singing tobacco, tobacco . . .
If anything she senses the sea
in the steady throb of the overworked
air conditioner, in the bright waves
of light bouncing from the lamp,
sweeping over the dining table,
the several enormous laundry baskets,
the pink shell that serves as an ashtray.

RETURN VISIT

After they were all gone
he sat in the old room and imagined her
sitting in the half-light as the moon rose,
higher, and now came clear through the door
left open, came across the floor very softly
to touch the back of the chair.
There was an open book on the table, books
everywhere, nothing but books
and a torn matchbook marked the place
where she had stopped . . .
just like those books he thought
and he wanted to speak to her
as people never speak to one another.
He wanted to say and hear the things
one never says and hears. He wanted
to know about the old woman's youth,
when the darkness moved about him
and around the chair one of the cats
came and pushed against his foot,
rubbing against his leg, purring.
Outside it grew light, almost like day,
but whiter, and he wondered if out there
one might be another thing altogether.

WE WHO NEED SORROW

When, around nine, night falls hard as buckshot,
the smoking stars, the cigarettes,
glow in the inexhaustible sky. Drunk,
in the folding chair, you give yourself entirely
to the gramophone. The radiant sprinkler
runs on in the dark. At the Arcadia Ballroom,
mad-eyed girls dance till their breath is gone.
Boys talk cars and wait for the right moment
to lead or follow. It's warm in Omaha,
there's music. Walking in his necktie,
Tony Sorrentino hums "Tuxedo Junction," then
thumbs the highway, blue for Eileen. It's
strange to love. You wind up talking to the moon.
If pears could be dreams, you're holding an opal.
Every song brings back Astronomy. God knows
the stars keep singing and your sons will learn
to drink. The gold timepiece you'll give
to the oldest, and for the young one
you'll go deaf a hundred times.

CITY LIFE

In the morning, we rise and dress without talking,
in separate rooms, deliberately not looking at each other,
not even noticing the splendid sun creeping
over the trellis, across the window,

the barges sliding and thumping down the river.
And of course, the piano, always obstructing
our view of one another (she never plays
the same song), a last cigarette broken,
dangling from her lip.

Now she steps to the balcony, watering the geraniums,
almost oblivious to the intentional slam of the door. Does she hear
the sound of my footsteps fading in the stairwell?
Halfway up the street,

pigeons lifting off an empty sidewalk, the traffic
on 72nd, meandering. As I wait for the bus, overhead
the silent wind moving the clouds away,
a newspaper turning in half-circles,
like one of the pigeons.

SOLDIERS

for Bill Kittredge

Our rifles sit like dogs on their hind legs.
We will be burying the dead in a minute.
Everyone is silent. How will I be able
to look at them. It's a deep grave
and the first soldiers get into it.
All of them have new boots.
They are dead and we drink wine.

The last shell over the trenches
opens like a flower. Tomorrow I might be lying
with my arms stretched out. If only my coat
would fit. So what if I look bad.
The fingers themselves unbutton the coat.
I'm shaving in front of a broken
piece of mirror. Why am I shaving?

I hear a typewriter clicking, it's only
rifle fire. I throw myself down.
There is an explosion, a short one.
Then, the song of an automatic, the staccato
of a submachine gun. The radioman is dead.
He caught a bullet right in the mouth.
It was a weak bullet, but it managed to kill him.

JACOB'S SONG

As she walks along the broken oyster shell road,
toward the sea, toward the shadowy wharf,
the wind fluttering the edge of her blue calico skirt,
she recalls Jacob, the sound of the ship's horn,
the rattle of the winches, the warm smell
of the engine room, the hull breaking the waves,
sorrow after sorrow. The moon seems far away,
the clouds like dark wings, rushing over the horizon.
In the near silence, she hears him talking alone with the stars,
his words like the sound of the lapping water,
and she is remembering him on the wharf,
as his voice continues to rise and fall,
and she gently lays her hands where he stood,
where she believed he would never leave. Then she hikes her skirt
to keep it out of the tidal wash, and walks over the last rise,
retracing her steps in the direction of her home.

FIRST DAY OF RAIN

Long after midnight, the rain holds us
sleepless like a cold kiss.
We know every tree in this forest.
There are no boundaries. Maria,
a woman I've never seen before,
turns her head one way, then another,
like a rhapsody. I watch the shadow
press a long fingermark on her forehead.
Perhaps she is dreaming owls across a field
where snakes grow nervous. Perhaps
she is afraid our words might let loose
against the quiet night. I want
to ask her if she believes in the quality
of the rain. Will we awake
to a knife of sunshine in water?
In some forest, a tree is falling. At last
the earth lets go. This is where
we begin ourselves.

WHERE THE ROAD ENDS

We enter a grove of useless trees,
where the only sound rolls in.
The horses, indifferent, breathe
submissively. Maria chants
the dark rosary, a centipede
falling from her hands.
I follow the guitar
bouncing about drunk
on the flanks of the horse.

The horses zigzag through
the trees, their shadows
surround us. Every tree
is a passing memory.
I have one joy . . .
to sing under my breath.
Better to close my eyes,
enjoy these moments
stolen from the night.

A FINE DAY FOR DRIVING

You woke dreaming those glasses soft
on the table. The one filled with lilacs
and the empty one. Admit it, you were crazy
for love. There's too much sorrow in Omaha.
The road threads through hills easy to trust.
The road could give a damn. Isn't it time
to swerve toward the stars?
Take the next turn for boyhood's sake.
If the sky unfolds like an open net,
if the wind complains, keep it to yourself.
And no one, no one will know how you left
without a word, and in your brown suit.

HOUND OF HEAVEN

At this moment there is a man standing
in the doorway across the street
who has been shadowing me for the past week.
His name is Gomez. He lives on stale toast
and sour milk. In the darkness of night
he unfastens his shoes.

The park is crowded with spectators. Fear keeps
me cold. The police vans turn away and start off
in another direction. I am lost in the black shapes
of trees.

At the end of the hallway I hear his hurried steps.
Something reminds me of myself and I turn.
It works like a prayer. Christ, my eyes.
Everywhere I look there is the movement of dreams.

THE WAY WATER DEVELOPS

Imagine you've never been anywhere else.
I've left the curtains open, the cellar is filling
with water. You overlook everything.
The sky flies up in a swarm of black.
"Anyone here?" you call, and pull
the electric switch. Words are nothing more
than currents of air. You will go
to a higher spot. Slowly, you begin to climb.

Now your shadow curls over the stair. I wait
to see if you try the locked room.
The water takes on a life of its own.
"Nothing must change," I whisper.
You will stay here. Everything must remain.

I have forgotten how to speak.
It's all in the mind. Meaningless. Here,
in the shell of bone, the skull.
I take the key from the lock and push the door
open. If the whole world came in I would not mind.
If the whole world came in,
would that leave room for me?

WHAT WAS NEEDED AT CEDAR BEACH, 1956

This photograph brings you back to a sky churning
with seagulls. There's Alfredo still fishing.
Poor fool, forever tangled in his line. Waves lost their color
and Maria's hat faded to nothing. They're depending
on the pier. That's how lives develop.
To one side, a gull nibbles at a squid Alfredo
counted on. Maria, his little dream, motionless.
She loved him for the odds and ends fished
out of his sweater. She loved his lean cold body
smelling of sea. Not even the crease across her shoulder
can change that.

ELEGY AT SUNSET BAY

Three miles from the nearest town,
a rogue wave crashes on the shore.
My mother has died.

Mid-air, a wayward gull shifts obliquely
where the sky meets the horizon.

One fallen tree, a broken antler
juts across the outlet
as Big Creek spills into the ocean.

To the south, the cliffs, strictly angular,
no romance, just hard stone,
sharp and unforgiving.

A group of sanderlings advances
and retreats in rhythm
with each wave.

I come to this place to remember
and to forget.

BASTENDORFF BEACH

Rocks—old relics from the brisk
Oregon coast. The sea—great winged
and white carried right to my feet.
Each wave deposits the small gift
then quickly snatches it back.

One outcrop looks like a whale's backbone,
bleached brilliantly white, or the spine
and ribs of a long gone galleon
floundering in the sea grass.

The long arm of the jetty
stretches toward the sea,
the sentinel light at Cape Arago,
blinks, then spins softly in the mist.

In the shoals infested with full beds
of urchin, every delicate creature's
a flower in itself.

The ocean has the same intricacy
as the sky, yet as I look into the waves
they're dying and being replaced.

THE MUSE

for Richard Robbins

On the shaded lanai,
slumped in a well worn rataan chair,
I look out to the open sea and Molokai,
to the gaze of a child-faced woman
in the open market holding the light of the morning
in a papaya. I know that I know The Muse as she dances
across the Lahaina marketplace in her red and white calico dress,
then turns for a moment and disappears in the crowd.
I spend the rest of the day reinventing her name over
and over again—Lalani, Halia, Kaikala.
Later, in the starlight of the Outrigger Hotel, The Muse reappears,
her black hair shimmering, waving her hands and golden bracelets.
Maybe it is just as well that she will not recognize me.
I think of the two red dragons on my writing desk, and
ask for some sign of strength.

NIGHT MUSIC

for George Cork Maul

Toward dawn, the light coming in over the mountains
turns the sky purple, and I look up, and realize that
I am alone. Last night you were talking about
how no one speaks, how we keep our words to ourselves
so that no one can find us. You could tell the words upset me,
as they sometimes will, and you drew close to me for a while,
your eyes shining in the darkness, almost as bright as the moon.
When I was 20 I heard a man play "Round Midnight"
sweet on the trumpet. In a pinstriped suit this black man
held the horn like a soulful woman, romanced every note
into the night air, and I heard for awhile, the echoing
song of Orpheus.

HOMAGE TO DRAKE AT CAPE ARAGO

for Rosemary Wakeman

> We dropped behind this headland in a bad bay
> through the vile thicke and stinking fogs.
>
> —*Sir Francis Drake, June 1579*

Why this place so desolate? Cold water, cold stone,
hard and angular, unforgiving, more like a grave than a monument.
It's true beauty hangs like mist in the trees each morning
though I doubt you noticed the slanting pines,
the Spanish moss.

Did you get close enough to latitude, the gleam of your sextent
searching for another meridian, listening to the song
of the sirens, the music of the Golden Hinde's running
rigging, the parrels sliding up and down,
shrouds pulling at the deadeyes, sails opening
like the wings of a soaring gull?
As you gazed off the starboard side
were you surprised, as I am, by the floating sunstars,
their deep red glow beneath the water,
warning you not to stay too long, not too long?

Still from this vantage point, the view seems right.
Is it wrong to idle in tidal pools rich with urchin
and anemone so pink it hurts my eyes
where the brilliant blue sky has no borders
except for the thin invisible line of the sea,
and waves explode haphazardly on broken rocks?
Does my life somehow resemble this trail
rambling on the cliff's side, down to a beach
littered with fossils?

AT LINDBERGH'S GRAVE, MAUI

for Lex Runciman

As the road veers away from the sea, away
from the surging tourists, the condominiums,
we thread toward Hana, through bamboo forests,
and almost miss the pull-off breaking into palmettos,
the simple Palapala Ho'omau church, the slate walkway
meandering to the graveyard.

Cement post openings lead to the older graves,
to the insignificant pale stone, it's incomplete inscription,
"If I take the wings of the morning, and dwell in the uttermost
parts of the sea . . ." A shimmering green gecko scuttles
across the nearby grave . . . your friend, Sam Pryor,
and his "children," the gibbons,
their cryptic names scrawled on slate—
Kikei, George, Lani, Kippy.
Two days was not enough time on this corner of paradise.

We are grateful for the gravedigger who convinced you
to let the wild plum live with you in spectral bloom,
who asked your pallbearers to wear their work clothes
as they passed the seven sacred pools, your casket
floating like a fuselage in mid-air.

LINDBERG ALOFT

The morning your plane lifted from Roosevelt Field,
you swerved over high trees, telephone lines,
a tractor suddenly red. You set your compass
due East while Long Island Sound faded away.
The gales of Newfoundland swept the Atlantic
with ice, shuttered the wings for 33 hours.
Without a moon, you thought of whisperings
and wing walking. Closing the throttle, your plane
passed a few feet from a fishing boat and you shouted,
"Which way is Ireland?" After Dingle Bay, Cape Valentia,
small English farms with stone walls, hedged fences,
and you thought no one knows what their home looks like
until they see it from above. In your final descent,
the coastline curved down from the North, and as you crossed
the channel, you flew over Cherbourg with the last light of the sun,
your heart racing, and you saw the lights of Paris.

LETTER FROM MONTANA

Your message came back uncancelled, except
for the 'sorry,' 'sorry,' each star sings
hard as sage in this man's prairie.
Love gave out with the railroad
miles away from Sacramento, or for that point,
St. Joseph. I left that place empty as a Jack Daniels
bottle. I left with an arsenal of violins.
The bartender said, "Come back in twenty years,
you'll do better." Like a lover I forgot the seasons.
The weak stayed, faded into houses
they call home. The weak live easily.
There's something they know
that we have forgotten. Our ears
should be open to the broken phonograph,
the town's silent music.
Where in Miles City is Stravinsky?
I'm coming to life again.
You'll receive this letter from Montana
where pain comes easy
and the water's enough to get you drunk.

BAD WEATHER

I'm forty miles from someone's town
driving through driving rain,
trying to forget the world's forever.
Goodbye to the gutters dark and deep
with leaves, goodbye to Aunt Emily
and small schoolhouse pranks.
I hope the phone keeps ringing.
I'm clear out of answers.

The radio died last week, this tune
will have to do. There's a beer
every ten miles and the highway
might never end. Not like Shelly
and the reverend's son—took off
in the middle of a dream.

Whatever I felt has gone to rain
and trees pass by like empty words.
It's twenty to one, and at two
I cross the county line. The map's
thick with lines and towns
with other colors.

A MAP OF MONTANA IN MIAMI

for Richard Hugo

Forgive the details. Those small errors
are waves. They drove the cartographer
insane. He managed this final dream.
That's him. The one who drinks too much,
the one who ships out in a bottle.
Say, "Noah" and glance back at the sea.

Everything became sound. He built
a boat without purpose, a measure between
two whales. He whistled "goodbye,"
and youth passed like a wing, buckling
in mid-air.

On the fortieth meridian they're fishing
for blues. Note the sand. That's part of
the legend. The lady in the wind tunnel
talks in the past. Gulls intercept themselves.
Thirty Ave Maria's.

THE DEMISE OF THE BEAVER HILL MINE

for Dick of the Storms

They called for a show of hands in '26.
All but the company watchman voted
to disincorporate. He stayed on forty years,
watching the buildings and wharves dissolve.

You'd never know this town had ten good years.
Mining dreams was the principal occupation.
Coal stayed King like no tomorrow, then
went bust at 600 tons.

The day the mine gave out failure turned green
with greed. Wives grew tired of days
in desperation, and absence fell short
of delivering anyone fondness.

Locals still talk about the big explosion,
the hotel reduced to a single hanging bulb,
flanked by stars on either side.

Whole neighborhoods abandoned, empty houses
reigned for years. Evelyn O'Malley ran away
with the Postmaster. Errant letters going
to who knows where.

EMPIRE, WHERE DREAMS DISSOLVE

Today the sea seems misaligned. Tourists watch waves
from their cars, and fingerlings glow greedy
with silver. You love this town for what it was,
and what it could have been. Once streets were paved
with Douglas Fir and miners dreamed of El Dorado.
Is this how dreams dissolve, in broken shouts
across the Hollering Place? Is this the day you know the palsied boy
who leans across the dock and can't remember your name?

At the 5 & 10 apathy is still on sale, sunglasses go out of style
on the carousel. There are whole neighborhoods where no one
speaks, and The Star of Hope brings no one redemption.
In the Silver Dollar they play for high stakes—Imagination
will always trump Memory. Maybe Seiver Lewis deserved
to swing from that alder, and the sound of the surf came roaring back.

The little theatre has one long running show. Woodpeckers
use the church for drilling practice. Wasn't it in that rambling
moonlight Anna Marie lost her virginity? They launched
a full investigation. She spent thirty years listening
to the sound of a broken buoy. At 67, the tide forgets to change.
Gulls alter their flight, lift their wings, then lift them again.
Their cries keep coming back, *mea culpa, mea culpa.*

SEQUEL

1

The river has a life apart
from the wind,
but the wind
dances elegantly.

2

I hear the wind
teaching the trees
to imitate birds
—and the leaves
suddenly take flight.

3

I'd rather watch the birds than write.
What a maddening gift
that they have to sing.

4

Like a fox,
with iodine red hands,
I want to taste of life itself.

EARLY OCTOBER

Near my home the trees flow northward
with the river broken by farms gentle and green.

    Each morning opens like a window
of bright manzanita. In the doorway of my father's house, I stand
between my body and the body of the land.

In the shadow under the alder tree, a bluejay nods
like any bluejay does. The river, loosely strung, seems to descend
from the watercolor on my wall—Andrew Wyeth's "Early October."

    Downstream, in shallow water, fish are lying
in pockets with a sandy bottom. Soon they're taking nymphs
beneath the surface, humping water toward the invisible.

There's only my voice no longer heard and the stars
    darkening one by one.
The spines of night fish stay intact, indifferent, they know
    only regret,
the shifting of bones.

THE PHOTOGRAPHER'S DREAM

Consider this a tinplate, a daguerreotype.
The woman holding the umbrella is barely recognizable,
and the shutter speed, inconsequential. You wonder
who she might be, and why after all these years,
the wind still flutters the edge of her pale cotton gown.
In the distance, the mountains appear ragged and undefined,
the ghost of a train fading from sepia to dull brown.
Isn't this when you understand that you will be holding
this image for the rest of your life? The garden spiders are already
spinning their webs, the trees lifting their shaggy heads.
As the evening lights go out in the valley, she unfastens her gown,
then loses herself in the cool night, across the unimaginable
blue sounds of Lester Young, the broken light of the kerosene lamp,
the little watercolor of Jesus with the lambs.

ANOTHER DAY

for Gerald McCrea

Late afternoon, no one's here,
the kind of day that comes without a thought,
when the heat ripples over the rhubarb patch,
and swarms of black flies rise from the melons.

Halfway across Johnson's pasture, the landscape drifts yellow
with yarrow, horses nose to nose at the salt lick, the scree
of a red tailed hawk.

There's nothing like the sliver of moon above a spreading tree,
sparrows that awake in flurries, knowing that the long drone
of the cicada, the insistent locust, might be enough to bring on
a storm. When the needles on a slash pine start to blow, the flick
of the wind brushes the branches, shakes the fretwork of thorny
vines, scatters the acorns.

There are moments when I understand why I am here,
like the inimitable whistle of an osprey. Where the road
turns away, the spiky heads of a sword fern burst
from an old tire, and two young wood rats emerge, blinking.

THE FISH AND THE MOON

March, the wind tangles the empty branches,
shakes the trees, blows the last remnants of leaves
to every corner of the yard. The moon is still hanging around,
like some transient, peeking through the window shades,
over the casement, across the livingroom carpet,
settling on our mahogany bookshelf,
where the Thai fighting fish, elegantly blue
in its glass jar, holds its anger.

HARVEST

The night sky opens its starry picture book: an archer,
a bear, a winged horse. And a thousand miles east, in North Platte,
I know you see them too. The house is empty, only the coffee rings
from yesterday's breakfast, lingering on the kitchen table.
It helps to remember we live in a lush garden,
no reason to act like wrens, arguing over sunflower seeds,
when the yard is full of thimbleberries, the wind gently
blowing millet to who knows where,
while the summer squash, already waiting by the sink,
glows golden and green, more than we will ever need.